I0617249

TABLE OF CONTENTS

HOW TO USE
THIS READING PLAN

This Bible Reading Plan is a 23-week chronological reading of all four Gospels exploring the birth, life, death, resurrection, and ascension of Jesus the Messiah. Each week is presented with several passages of Scripture revolving around one unique theme that emerges from Jesus' life as seen in the writings of Matthew, Mark, Luke, and John. These stories are based on a condensed timeline of the entirety of Jesus' life from His birth on earth to His ascension into Heaven.

The three criteria that went into the development of this reading plan are:

- **Chronology** – The recorded events in the timeline of Jesus' life on earth.
- **Theme** – Some of the big ideas or "headlines" that emerge from those recorded events.
- **Harmony** – A synthesis of Scriptural passages from all four Gospels where those events are referenced.

This 23-week devotional is organized as a 3-volume set. Volume 1 is eight weeks long and covers the early years of the life of Jesus. Volume 2 covers the middle years of Jesus' public ministry over seven weeks. Volume 3 covers the final years of Jesus' public ministry and is eight weeks.

Our desire is that as you read the story of Jesus through the Gospels, His life unfolds before you like a binge-worthy drama that connects historical chronology to patterns of our everyday lives. Ultimately, our prayer is for you to experience first-hand the living, resurrected Messiah King Jesus as the Chief Shepherd of your soul (1 Peter 2:25).

DAILY DEVOTIONAL AND JOURNAL

DAY 1

Feel free to journal about some of the things you feel like the Lord is doing in your life. You may also desire to bring this journal with you to a weekend worship experience and take notes on the sermon/message. During Days 2-6, we recommend you use the P.R.A.Y. Method:

DAY 2-6

Pray – Praying with Jesus. Begin your time of devotion with prayer. Use this pattern for prayer inspired by The Lord's Prayer (Matthew 6:5-15; Luke 11:1-13)

- **Praise** (*"Our Father, who is in Heaven..."*). Thank God for who He is and praise Him for the things He has done in your life.
- **Petitions** (*"Let Your Kingdom come..."*). Ask the Lord for specific things to be done in the world, your life, and in the lives of others.
- **Proclamations** (*"Yours is the Kingdom and the Power and the Glory..."*). End your time of prayer with a proclamation of God's rule, reign, and sovereignty.

Read – Reading about Jesus. Write about verses that stand out as you go through the Gospel readings. As you read, try to keep a few questions in mind:
- Who is speaking?
- Who is being spoken to?
- What could this potentially mean for my life today?

Ask – Asking for guidance from Jesus. Spend time asking the Lord for wisdom and insight as you meditate on what you prayed and the Scriptures you read. A good practice is to ask the Holy Spirit — who Jesus promised would "teach you all things" (John 14:26) — to teach you something about the life of Jesus that day.

Yield – Yielding our will to Jesus. Take time throughout your day to intentionally yield to the Lord and demonstrate Christ-likeness in your daily life. Write out some ways you are becoming like Jesus each day.

DAY 7

Day 7 ends with a time of Sabbath rest, reflection, and the opportunity to catch up on any missed readings from that week.

OVERVIEW OF THE WEEKLY READINGS FROM "23" VOLUME 3

**OUR PRAYER FOR YOU
AS YOU ENGAGE IN
THIS DAILY JOURNEY
WITH JESUS THROUGH
THE GOSPELS:**

SPEND TIME WITH JESUS

LEARN FROM JESUS

BECOME MORE LIKE JESUS

THE TRIUMPHAL ENTRY

WEEK: 1	WEEKLY MEMORY VERSE:
	So they took branches of palm trees and went out to meet him, crying out, "Hosanna! Blessed is he who comes in the name of the Lord, even the King of Israel! " - **John 12:13**
TODAY'S READING: **John 12:1-50**	

PRAY: Take time to bring praise, petitions and/or proclamations to the Lord today.

READ: What are some Scriptures or stories that stood out to you today?

ASK: What's something the Holy Spirit wants you to learn about Jesus today?

YIELD: What are some ways that you can (or did) yield to the Lord today?

WEEK: 1	WEEKLY MEMORY VERSE:
TODAY'S READING: # Matthew 21:1-46	*So they took branches of palm trees and went out to meet him, crying out, "Hosanna! Blessed is he who comes in the name of the Lord, even the King of Israel!"* - **John 12:13**

PRAY: Take time to bring praise, petitions and/or proclamations to the Lord today.

READ: What are some Scriptures or stories that stood out to you today?

ASK: What's something the Holy Spirit wants you to learn about Jesus today?

YIELD: What are some ways that you can (or did) yield to the Lord today?

WEEK: 1	WEEKLY MEMORY VERSE:
TODAY'S READING: # Luke 18:1-43	*So they took branches of palm trees and went out to meet him, crying out, "Hosanna! Blessed is he who comes in the name of the Lord, even the King of Israel! "* - **John 12:13**

PRAY: Take time to bring praise, petitions and/or proclamations to the Lord today.

READ: What are some Scriptures or stories that stood out to you today?

ASK: What's something the Holy Spirit wants you to learn about Jesus today?

YIELD: What are some ways that you can (or did) yield to the Lord today?

WEEK: 1	WEEKLY MEMORY VERSE:
TODAY'S READING:	*So they took branches of palm trees and went out to meet him, crying out, "Hosanna! Blessed is he who comes in the name of the Lord, even the King of Israel!"* - **John 12:13**
# Mark 15:1-32	

PRAY: Take time to bring praise, petitions and/or proclamations to the Lord today.

READ: What are some Scriptures or stories that stood out to you today?

ASK: What's something the Holy Spirit wants you to learn about Jesus today?

YIELD: What are some ways that you can (or did) yield to the Lord today?

WEEK: 1	WEEKLY MEMORY VERSE:
TODAY'S READING: # Mark 15:33-47	*So they took branches of palm trees and went out to meet him, crying out, "Hosanna! Blessed is he who comes in the name of the Lord, even the King of Israel! "* - **John 12:13**

PRAY: Take time to bring praise, petitions and/or proclamations to the Lord today.

READ: What are some Scriptures or stories that stood out to you today?

ASK: What's something the Holy Spirit wants you to learn about Jesus today?

YIELD: What are some ways that you can (or did) yield to the Lord today?

WEEK: 1	WEEKLY MEMORY VERSE:
RECAP OF WEEK 1 SCRIPTURES: Mon - John 12:1-50 Tues - Matthew 21:1-46 Wed - Luke 18:1-43 Thur - Mark 15:1-32 Fri - Mark 15:33-47	*So they took branches of palm trees and went out to meet him, crying out, "Hosanna! Blessed is he who comes in the name of the Lord, even the King of Israel! "* - **John 12:13**

REST: What are some ways that I can rest in the Lord today?

REFLECT: What are some things that I learned about the life of Jesus—and myself—this week?

THE RESURRECTION

WEEK: 2	WEEKLY MEMORY VERSE:
	And he said to them, "Do not be alarmed. You seek Jesus of Nazareth, who was crucified. He has risen; he is not here. See the place where they laid him." - **Mark 16:6**
TODAY'S READING: **Mark 16:1-13**	

PRAY: Take time to bring praise, petitions and/or proclamations to the Lord today.

READ: What are some Scriptures or stories that stood out to you today?

ASK: What's something the Holy Spirit wants you to learn about Jesus today?

YIELD: What are some ways that you can (or did) yield to the Lord today?

WEEK: 2	**WEEKLY MEMORY VERSE:**
	And he said to them, "Do not be alarmed.
TODAY'S READING:	*You seek Jesus of Nazareth, who was*
	crucified. He has risen; he is not here. See
Matthew 22:1-46	*the place where they laid him." -* **Mark 16:6**

PRAY: Take time to bring praise, petitions and/or proclamations to the Lord today.

READ: What are some Scriptures or stories that stood out to you today?

ASK: What's something the Holy Spirit wants you to learn about Jesus today?

YIELD: What are some ways that you can (or did) yield to the Lord today?

WEEK: 2	WEEKLY MEMORY VERSE:
	And he said to them, "Do not be alarmed.
TODAY'S READING:	*You seek Jesus of Nazareth, who was*
	crucified. He has risen; he is not here. See
# John 13:1-38	*the place where they laid him." -* **Mark 16:6**

PRAY: Take time to bring praise, petitions and/or proclamations to the Lord today.

READ: What are some Scriptures or stories that stood out to you today?

ASK: What's something the Holy Spirit wants you to learn about Jesus today?

YIELD: What are some ways that you can (or did) yield to the Lord today?

WEEK: 2	WEEKLY MEMORY VERSE:
	And he said to them, "Do not be alarmed. You seek Jesus of Nazareth, who was crucified. He has risen; he is not here. See the place where they laid him." - **Mark 16:6**
TODAY'S READING:	
# Luke 19:1-27	

PRAY: Take time to bring praise, petitions and/or proclamations to the Lord today.

READ: What are some Scriptures or stories that stood out to you today?

ASK: What's something the Holy Spirit wants you to learn about Jesus today?

YIELD: What are some ways that you can (or did) yield to the Lord today?

WEEK: 2	WEEKLY MEMORY VERSE:
	And he said to them, "Do not be alarmed. You seek Jesus of Nazareth, who was crucified. He has risen; he is not here. See the place where they laid him." - **Mark 16:6**
TODAY'S READING:	
Luke 19:28-48	

PRAY: Take time to bring praise, petitions and/or proclamations to the Lord today.

READ: What are some Scriptures or stories that stood out to you today?

ASK: What's something the Holy Spirit wants you to learn about Jesus today?

YIELD: What are some ways that you can (or did) yield to the Lord today?

WEEK: 2	WEEKLY MEMORY VERSE:
	*And he said to them, "Do not be alarmed. You seek Jesus of Nazareth, who was crucified. He has risen; he is not here. See the place where they laid him." - **Mark 16:6***
RECAP OF WEEK 2 SCRIPTURES: Mon - Mark 16:1-13 Tues - Matthew 22:1-46 Wed - John 13:1-38 Thur - Luke 19:1-27 Fri - Luke 19:28-48	

REST: What are some ways that I can rest in the Lord today?

REFLECT: What are some things that I learned about the life of Jesus—and myself—this week?

THE WAY, TRUTH AND LIFE

WEEK: 3

WEEK: 3	WEEKLY MEMORY VERSE:
	Jesus said to him, "I am the way, and the truth, and the life. No one comes to the Father except through me." - John 14:6
TODAY'S READING: John 14:1-31	

PRAY: Take time to bring praise, petitions and/or proclamations to the Lord today.

READ: What are some Scriptures or stories that stood out to you today?

ASK: What's something the Holy Spirit wants you to learn about Jesus today?

YIELD: What are some ways that you can (or did) yield to the Lord today?

WEEK: 3	**WEEKLY MEMORY VERSE:**
	Jesus said to him, "I am the way, and the truth, and the life. No one comes to the Father except through me." - John 14:6
TODAY'S READING: **Matthew 23:1-12**	

PRAY: Take time to bring praise, petitions and/or proclamations to the Lord today.

READ: What are some Scriptures or stories that stood out to you today?

ASK: What's something the Holy Spirit wants you to learn about Jesus today?

YIELD: What are some ways that you can (or did) yield to the Lord today?

WEEK: 3	WEEKLY MEMORY VERSE:
	Jesus said to him, "I am the way, and the truth, and the life. No one comes to the Father except through me." - John 14:6
TODAY'S READING: **Matthew 23:13-39**	

PRAY: Take time to bring praise, petitions and/or proclamations to the Lord today.

READ: What are some Scriptures or stories that stood out to you today?

ASK: What's something the Holy Spirit wants you to learn about Jesus today?

YIELD: What are some ways that you can (or did) yield to the Lord today?

WEEK: 3	WEEKLY MEMORY VERSE:
	Jesus said to him, "I am the way, and the truth, and the life. No one comes to the Father except through me." - John 14:6
TODAY'S READING: **Luke 20:1-27**	

PRAY: Take time to bring praise, petitions and/or proclamations to the Lord today.

READ: What are some Scriptures or stories that stood out to you today?

ASK: What's something the Holy Spirit wants you to learn about Jesus today?

YIELD: What are some ways that you can (or did) yield to the Lord today?

WEEK: 3	WEEKLY MEMORY VERSE:
	Jesus said to him, "I am the way, and the truth, and the life. No one comes to the Father except through me." - John 14:6
TODAY'S READING:	
# Luke 20:28-47	

PRAY: Take time to bring praise, petitions and/or proclamations to the Lord today.

READ: What are some Scriptures or stories that stood out to you today?

ASK: What's something the Holy Spirit wants you to learn about Jesus today?

YIELD: What are some ways that you can (or did) yield to the Lord today?

WEEK: 3	WEEKLY MEMORY VERSE:
	Jesus said to him, "I am the way, and the truth, and the life. No one comes to the Father except through me."
RECAP OF WEEK 3 SCRIPTURES:	- **John 14:6**
Mon - John 14:1-31 Tues - Matthew 23:1-12 Wed - Matthew 23:13-39 Thur - Luke 20:1-27 Fri - Luke 20:28-47	

REST: What are some ways that I can rest in the Lord today?

REFLECT: What are some things that I learned about the life of Jesus—and myself—this week?

ABIDE

WEEK: 4	WEEKLY MEMORY VERSE:
	"I am the vine; you are the branches. Whoever abides in me and I in him, he it is that bears much fruit, for apart from me you can do nothing."
TODAY'S READING:	
John 15:1-27	- John 15:5

PRAY: Take time to bring praise, petitions and/or proclamations to the Lord today.

READ: What are some Scriptures or stories that stood out to you today?

ASK: What's something the Holy Spirit wants you to learn about Jesus today?

YIELD: What are some ways that you can (or did) yield to the Lord today?

WEEK: 4	WEEKLY MEMORY VERSE:
	"I am the vine; you are the branches. Whoever abides in me and I in him, he it is that bears much fruit, for apart from me you can do nothing."
TODAY'S READING:	- John 15:5
# John 16:1-33	

PRAY: Take time to bring praise, petitions and/or proclamations to the Lord today.

READ: What are some Scriptures or stories that stood out to you today?

ASK: What's something the Holy Spirit wants you to learn about Jesus today?

YIELD: What are some ways that you can (or did) yield to the Lord today?

WEEK: 4	WEEKLY MEMORY VERSE:
	"I am the vine; you are the branches. Whoever abides in me and I in him, he it is that bears much fruit, for apart from me you can do nothing." - John 15:5
TODAY'S READING: # Matthew 24:1-28	

PRAY: Take time to bring praise, petitions and/or proclamations to the Lord today.

READ: What are some Scriptures or stories that stood out to you today?

ASK: What's something the Holy Spirit wants you to learn about Jesus today?

YIELD: What are some ways that you can (or did) yield to the Lord today?

WEEK: 4	WEEKLY MEMORY VERSE:
	"I am the vine; you are the branches. Whoever abides in me and I in him, he it is that bears much fruit, for apart from me you can do nothing." - John 15:5
TODAY'S READING: **Matthew 24:29-51**	

PRAY: Take time to bring praise, petitions and/or proclamations to the Lord today.

READ: What are some Scriptures or stories that stood out to you today?

ASK: What's something the Holy Spirit wants you to learn about Jesus today?

YIELD: What are some ways that you can (or did) yield to the Lord today?

WEEK: 4	WEEKLY MEMORY VERSE:
	"I am the vine; you are the branches. Whoever abides in me and I in him, he it is that bears much fruit, for apart from me you can do nothing." - John 15:5
TODAY'S READING: Luke 21:1-38	

PRAY: Take time to bring praise, petitions and/or proclamations to the Lord today.

READ: What are some Scriptures or stories that stood out to you today?

ASK: What's something the Holy Spirit wants you to learn about Jesus today?

YIELD: What are some ways that you can (or did) yield to the Lord today?

WEEK: 4	WEEKLY MEMORY VERSE:
	"I am the vine; you are the branches. Whoever abides in me and I in him, he it is that bears much fruit, for apart from me you can do nothing."
RECAP OF WEEK 4 SCRIPTURES:	- **John 15:5**
Mon - John 15:1-27 Tues - John 16:1-33 Wed - Matthew 24:1-28 Thur - Matthew 24:29-51 Fri - Luke 1-38	

REST: What are some ways that I can rest in the Lord today?

REFLECT: What are some things that I learned about the life of Jesus—and myself—this week?

SENT

WEEK: 5

WEEK: 5	WEEKLY MEMORY VERSE:
	"Sanctify them in the truth; your word is truth. As you sent me into the world, so I have sent them into the world." - John 17:17-18
TODAY'S READING: John 17:1-26	

PRAY: Take time to bring praise, petitions and/or proclamations to the Lord today.

READ: What are some Scriptures or stories that stood out to you today?

ASK: What's something the Holy Spirit wants you to learn about Jesus today?

YIELD: What are some ways that you can (or did) yield to the Lord today?

WEEK: 5	WEEKLY MEMORY VERSE:
	"Sanctify them in the truth; your word is truth. As you sent me into the world, so I have sent them into the world."
TODAY'S READING:	- John 17:17-18
# John 18:1-40	

PRAY: Take time to bring praise, petitions and/or proclamations to the Lord today.

READ: What are some Scriptures or stories that stood out to you today?

ASK: What's something the Holy Spirit wants you to learn about Jesus today?

YIELD: What are some ways that you can (or did) yield to the Lord today?

WEEKLY MEMORY VERSE:

"Sanctify them in the truth; your word is truth. As you sent me into the world, so I have sent them into the world."
- John 17:17-18

TODAY'S READING:

Luke 22:1-71

PRAY: Take time to bring praise, petitions and/or proclamations to the Lord today.

READ: What are some Scriptures or stories that stood out to you today?

ASK: What's something the Holy Spirit wants you to learn about Jesus today?

YIELD: What are some ways that you can (or did) yield to the Lord today?

WEEK: 5	WEEKLY MEMORY VERSE:
	"Sanctify them in the truth; your word is truth. As you sent me into the world, so I have sent them into the world."
TODAY'S READING:	- John 17:17-18
# Matthew 25:1-46	

PRAY: Take time to bring praise, petitions and/or proclamations to the Lord today.

READ: What are some Scriptures or stories that stood out to you today?

ASK: What's something the Holy Spirit wants you to learn about Jesus today?

YIELD: What are some ways that you can (or did) yield to the Lord today?

WEEK: 5	WEEKLY MEMORY VERSE:
	"Sanctify them in the truth; your word is truth. As you sent me into the world, so I have sent them into the world." - John 17:17-18
TODAY'S READING: # Matthew 26:1-75	

PRAY: Take time to bring praise, petitions and/or proclamations to the Lord today.

READ: What are some Scriptures or stories that stood out to you today?

ASK: What's something the Holy Spirit wants you to learn about Jesus today?

YIELD: What are some ways that you can (or did) yield to the Lord today?

WEEK: 5	WEEKLY MEMORY VERSE:
	"Sanctify them in the truth; your word is truth. As you sent me into the world, so I have sent them into the world."
RECAP OF WEEK 5 SCRIPTURES: Mon - John 17:1-26 Tues - John 18:1-40 Wed - Luke 22:1-71 Thur - Matthew 25:1-46 Fri - Matthew 26:1-75	- **John 17:17-18**

REST: What are some ways that I can rest in the Lord today?

REFLECT: What are some things that I learned about the life of Jesus—and myself—this week?

IT IS FINISHED

WEEK: 6	WEEKLY MEMORY VERSE:
	When Jesus had received the sour wine, he said, "It is finished," and he bowed his head and gave up his spirit." - John 19:30
TODAY'S READING: John 19:1-42	

PRAY: Take time to bring praise, petitions and/or proclamations to the Lord today.

READ: What are some Scriptures or stories that stood out to you today?

ASK: What's something the Holy Spirit wants you to learn about Jesus today?

YIELD: What are some ways that you can (or did) yield to the Lord today?

WEEK: 6	WEEKLY MEMORY VERSE:
	When Jesus had received the sour wine, he said, "It is finished," and he bowed his head and gave up his spirit." - John 19:30
TODAY'S READING:	
# Luke 23:1-25	

PRAY: Take time to bring praise, petitions and/or proclamations to the Lord today.

READ: What are some Scriptures or stories that stood out to you today?

ASK: What's something the Holy Spirit wants you to learn about Jesus today?

YIELD: What are some ways that you can (or did) yield to the Lord today?

WEEK: 6	WEEKLY MEMORY VERSE:
	When Jesus had received the sour wine, he said, "It is finished," and he bowed his head and gave up his spirit." - John 19:30
TODAY'S READING: Luke 23:26-56	

PRAY: Take time to bring praise, petitions and/or proclamations to the Lord today.

READ: What are some Scriptures or stories that stood out to you today?

ASK: What's something the Holy Spirit wants you to learn about Jesus today?

YIELD: What are some ways that you can (or did) yield to the Lord today?

WEEK: 6	WEEKLY MEMORY VERSE:
	When Jesus had received the sour wine, he said, "It is finished," and he bowed his head and gave up his spirit." - John 19:30
TODAY'S READING: **Matthew 27:1-31**	

PRAY: Take time to bring praise, petitions and/or proclamations to the Lord today.

READ: What are some Scriptures or stories that stood out to you today?

ASK: What's something the Holy Spirit wants you to learn about Jesus today?

YIELD: What are some ways that you can (or did) yield to the Lord today?

WEEK: 6	WEEKLY MEMORY VERSE:
	When Jesus had received the sour wine, he said, "It is finished," and he bowed his head and gave up his spirit." - John 19:30
TODAY'S READING: **Matthew 27:32-66**	

PRAY: Take time to bring praise, petitions and/or proclamations to the Lord today.

READ: What are some Scriptures or stories that stood out to you today?

ASK: What's something the Holy Spirit wants you to learn about Jesus today?

YIELD: What are some ways that you can (or did) yield to the Lord today?

WEEK: 6	WEEKLY MEMORY VERSE:
	When Jesus had received the sour wine, he said, "It is finished," and he bowed his head and gave up his spirit." - **John 19:30**
RECAP OF WEEK 6 SCRIPTURES: Mon - John 19:1-42 Tues - Luke 23:1-25 Wed - Luke 23:26-56 Thur - Matthew 27:1-31 Fri - Matthew 27:32-66	

Rest: What are some ways that I can rest in the Lord today?

Reflect: What are some things that I learned about the life of Jesus—and myself—this week?

RESURRECTED
APPEARANCES

WEEK: 7	WEEKLY MEMORY VERSE:
	They said to each other, "Did not our hearts burn within us while he talked to us on the road, while he opened to us the Scriptures?" - **Luke 24:32**
TODAY'S READING: # Luke 24:1-32	

PRAY: Take time to bring praise, petitions and/or proclamations to the Lord today.

READ: What are some Scriptures or stories that stood out to you today?

ASK: What's something the Holy Spirit wants you to learn about Jesus today?

YIELD: What are some ways that you can (or did) yield to the Lord today?

WEEK: 7	WEEKLY MEMORY VERSE:
	They said to each other, "Did not our hearts burn within us while he talked to us on the road, while he opened to us the Scriptures?" - **Luke 24:32**
TODAY'S READING:	
Luke 24:33-49	

PRAY: Take time to bring praise, petitions and/or proclamations to the Lord today.

READ: What are some Scriptures or stories that stood out to you today?

ASK: What's something the Holy Spirit wants you to learn about Jesus today?

YIELD: What are some ways that you can (or did) yield to the Lord today?

WEEK: 7	WEEKLY MEMORY VERSE:
	They said to each other, "Did not our hearts burn within us while he talked to us on the road, while he opened to us the Scriptures?" - **Luke 24:32**
TODAY'S READING: # John 20:1-18	

PRAY: Take time to bring praise, petitions and/or proclamations to the Lord today.

READ: What are some Scriptures or stories that stood out to you today?

ASK: What's something the Holy Spirit wants you to learn about Jesus today?

YIELD: What are some ways that you can (or did) yield to the Lord today?

WEEK: 7	**WEEKLY MEMORY VERSE:**
	They said to each other, "Did not our hearts burn within us while he talked to us on the road, while he opened to us the Scriptures?" - **Luke 24:32**
TODAY'S READING: # John 20:19-31	

PRAY: Take time to bring praise, petitions and/or proclamations to the Lord today.

READ: What are some Scriptures or stories that stood out to you today?

ASK: What's something the Holy Spirit wants you to learn about Jesus today?

YIELD: What are some ways that you can (or did) yield to the Lord today?

WEEK: 7	WEEKLY MEMORY VERSE:
	They said to each other, "Did not our hearts burn within us while he talked to us on the road, while he opened to us the Scriptures?" - **Luke 24:32**
TODAY'S READING: **Matthew 28:1-15**	

PRAY: Take time to bring praise, petitions and/or proclamations to the Lord today.

READ: What are some Scriptures or stories that stood out to you today?

ASK: What's something the Holy Spirit wants you to learn about Jesus today?

YIELD: What are some ways that you can (or did) yield to the Lord today?

WEEK: 7	WEEKLY MEMORY VERSE:
	They said to each other, "Did not our hearts burn within us while he talked to us on the road, while he opened to us the Scriptures?" - **Luke 24:32**
RECAP OF WEEK 7 SCRIPTURES: Mon - Luke 24:1-32 Tues - Luke 24:33-49 Wed - John 20:1-18 Thur - John 20:19-31 Fri - Matthew 28:1-15	

REST: What are some ways that I can rest in the Lord today?

REFLECT: What are some things that I learned about the life of Jesus—and myself—this week?

GO AND MAKE DISCIPLES

WEEK: 8

NOTES:

WEEK: 8	WEEKLY MEMORY VERSE:
TODAY'S READING: # Matthew 28:16-20	*" Go therefore and make disciples of all nations, baptizing them in the name of the Father and of the Son and of the Holy Spirit, teaching them to observe all that I have commanded you. And behold, I am with you ways, to the end of the age."* - **Matthew 28:19-20**

PRAY: Take time to bring praise, petitions and/or proclamations to the Lord today.

READ: What are some Scriptures or stories that stood out to you today?

ASK: What's something the Holy Spirit wants you to learn about Jesus today?

YIELD: What are some ways that you can (or did) yield to the Lord today?

WEEK: 8	WEEKLY MEMORY VERSE:
TODAY'S READING: # Mark 16:14-20	*" Go therefore and make disciples of all nations, baptizing them in the name of the Father and of the Son and of the Holy Spirit, teaching them to observe all that I have commanded you. And behold, I am with you ways, to the end of the age."* - **Matthew 28:19-20**

PRAY: Take time to bring praise, petitions and/or proclamations to the Lord today.

READ: What are some Scriptures or stories that stood out to you today?

ASK: What's something the Holy Spirit wants you to learn about Jesus today?

YIELD: What are some ways that you can (or did) yield to the Lord today?

WEEK: 8	WEEKLY MEMORY VERSE:
	" Go therefore and make disciples of all nations, baptizing them in the name of the Father and of the Son and of the Holy Spirit, teaching them to observe all that I have commanded you. And behold, I am with you ways, to the end of the age."
TODAY'S READING:	
Luke 24:50-53	- Matthew 28:19-20

PRAY: Take time to bring praise, petitions and/or proclamations to the Lord today.

READ: What are some Scriptures or stories that stood out to you today?

ASK: What's something the Holy Spirit wants you to learn about Jesus today?

YIELD: What are some ways that you can (or did) yield to the Lord today?

WEEK: 8	WEEKLY MEMORY VERSE:
	" Go therefore and make disciples of all nations, baptizing them in the name of the Father and of the Son and of the Holy Spirit, teaching them to observe all that I have commanded you. And behold, I am with you ways, to the end of the age."
TODAY'S READING:	
John 21:1-14	- **Matthew 28:19-20**

PRAY: Take time to bring praise, petitions and/or proclamations to the Lord today.

READ: What are some Scriptures or stories that stood out to you today?

ASK: What's something the Holy Spirit wants you to learn about Jesus today?

YIELD: What are some ways that you can (or did) yield to the Lord today?

WEEK: 8	WEEKLY MEMORY VERSE:
TODAY'S READING: # John 21:15-25	" *Go therefore and make disciples of all nations, baptizing them in the name of the Father and of the Son and of the Holy Spirit, teaching them to observe all that I have commanded you. And behold, I am with you ways, to the end of the age.*" - **Matthew 28:19-20**

PRAY: Take time to bring praise, petitions and/or proclamations to the Lord today.

READ: What are some Scriptures or stories that stood out to you today?

ASK: What's something the Holy Spirit wants you to learn about Jesus today?

YIELD: What are some ways that you can (or did) yield to the Lord today?

WEEK: 8	WEEKLY MEMORY VERSE:
	" Go therefore and make disciples of all nations, baptizing them in the name of the Father and of the Son and of the Holy Spirit, teaching them to observe all that I have commanded you. And behold, I am with you ways, to the end of the age."
RECAP OF WEEK 7 SCRIPTURES: Mon - Matthew 28:16-20 Tues - Mark 16:14-20 Wed - Luke 24:50-53 Thur - John 21:1-14 Fri - John 21:15-25	- **Matthew 28:19-20**

REST: What are some ways that I can rest in the Lord today?

REFLECT: What are some things that I learned about the life of Jesus—and myself—this week?

THANK YOU FOR JOINING US ON THIS 23 WEEK JOURNEY.

www.ingramcontent.com/pod-product-compliance
Lightning Source LLC
Chambersburg PA
CBHW051653120626
46551CB00021B/2229